DAUGHTER IN THE HOUSE

People at Home

Also by Graham

OH SIDNEY—NOT THE WALNUT TREE: PEOPLE IN CARTOONS
TO THE OFFICE AND BACK: MORE PEOPLE IN CARTOONS
NORMALLY I NEVER TOUCH IT: PEOPLE AT PARTIES

DAUGHTER IN THE HOUSE

PEOPLE AT HOME

GEOFFREY BLES 1969

© ALEX GRAHAM, 1969

SBN: 7138 0247 2

Printed in Great Britain
by Cox & Wyman Ltd, Fakenham

Published by
Geoffrey Bles Ltd
52 Doughty Street, London, W.C.1
36–38 Clarence Street, Sydney
353 Elizabeth Street, Melbourne
246 Queen Street, Brisbane
CML Building, King William Street, Adelaide
Lake Road, Northcote, Auckland
100 Lesmill Road, Don Mills, Ontario
P.O. Box 8879, Johannesburg
P.O. Box 834, Cape Town
P.O. Box 2800, Salisbury, Rhodesia
First published September 1969
Reprinted October 1969

Contents

NOTE

These drawings originally appeared in Punch *and are reproduced
by permission of the magazine*

To Arran, the daughter in my house,
with love

DAUGHTER IN THE HOUSE

'I wonder any man alive will ever rear
a daughter.'

JOHN GAY, 1685–1732

So it's no new problem . . . Parents who have,
overnight it seems, seen their daughter transformed
from a lumpish schoolgirl into a sophisticated (and
by God, beautiful) young lady will know what this
book is about.

'For somebody who failed A-level French she doesn't seem to do at all badly!'

'She's lost her eye-lashes.'

'If it's Tim I never want to speak to him again . . . If it's Mickey I'm out . . . If it's Peter I'll ring him back . . . If it's Richard I'll take it.'

'Well?'

'It's not what I'd call
sensible underwear,
dear.'

'O don't worry about them—they can go to a cinema or something!'

*'If you could just give us some sort of **approximate** time when you might be home.'*

They will know the relief of hearing the car coming up the drive at 2 a.m. (she said she'd be home around eleven).

'Don't be late, dear.'

'For Heaven's sake stop saying "They may have had a puncture."'

'She's out!'

'*Good heavens no, dear—of course we weren't worried.*'

They will be familiar with those times when the paternal patience is strained to near breaking point . . .

'Seeing Granny's coming for tea don't you think you should put on your pretty pink dress?'

'Drinks in the sideboard, gang—I'll lay on some food.'

'I'd have thought you'd have invested in a dishwashing
machine by now.'

'Is this Frank Sinatra any relation of Nancy?'

'Oh that? . . . Well, coming home from the dance last
night, Roger—you know what fun Roger is—Roger said
"Let's . . ."'

'If you like, dear, I could help you tidy your room a little.'

'It was a very good dance. . . . I enjoyed it . . . I danced with lots of people
. . . the food was delicious . . . I got in about three . . . Robin Smith drove
me home . . .'

. . . and sometimes, if it comes to that, their daughter's too!

'Who's for Scrabble?'

'And this is my Father, Christopher.'

*'I get so **bored** with television.'*

And then there is the varied assortment of young men who appear on the doorstep . . .

'It's the one with glasses.'

'Gosh! You look stunning, Mrs. Macdermott.'

'Dad been looking after you all right?'

'I'm sure Timmy's people must be wondering where he's got to . . .'

. . . (they fancy non
of them as a potentia
son-in-law) . . .

*'If it's a red-haired boy on a Lambretta
I'm out!'*

*'I'm sure she'll be able to straighten it out when
she comes downstairs.'*

20

'Somehow Daddy and I had imagined Dirk as being a little—you know—younger.

. . . but to whom, of course, they are always pleased to offer hospitality.

*gars . . . brandy . . . all this! . . . Your old man must be loaded.'

'Actually, sir, I'd rather have a vodka and tonic if you have it.'

'Sir, I'm not Richard . . . I'm Jonathan.'

Cheerfully they put up with some minor inconveniences . . .

*'I don't **want** to go to the cinema!'*

' . . . and you plug in over here, Bill.'

... to please their darling daughter.

'Can we put up half a cricket team on Friday night?'

'This IS 27 Fernden Avenue, isn't it?'

'Top of the Pops?'

The family car is gladly shared . . .

'Darling, may we have the car tonight?'

'Hold it, hold it! I can't get my safety belt fastened!'

. . . though in the end they may have to buy her one of her own . . .

*'Imagine that, a second-hand mini . . . imagine Susan's parents giving her a second-hand mini for **her** birthday.'*

'Dad let me have the Rolls.'

. . . as so many other parents seem to have done!

'She's brought a few friends home, that's it.'

'Dad, may I have the car this evening?'

'We're not due at the Watsons till 7.30, dear.'

And, of course, the telephone . . .

*'I wonder if it's that nice boy whose father's a stockbroker and has
a Bentley and a house on Ibiza?'*

. . . is in constant use . . .

'It's for you.'

'It'll be Giles—he's taken a vacation job in an all-night café.'

'Sarah Howard, did you say?'

'His name's Bob, and he's ringing from a call box!'

... though sometimes under difficulties!

'Hold on a minute, Harry . . . we're fighting a losing battle here against the Bee Gees!'

'Where, dear? . . . Seven miles down the by-pass . . . it won't go . . . you think the engine's seized up . . . yes of course Daddy will turn out with the Austin . . .'

'I wonder if you'd care to have a glance at the telephone account?'

Apart from the telephone there are other drains on the income.

'We went mad!'

*'Approximately how much would this
ski-ing holiday cost?'*

*'Of **course** Daddy will buy one of Roger's paintings.'*

Pity, too, the poor father who may find himself the isolated victim of a well-organized female conspiracy.

'I quite agree, dear . . . I would have changed down for that corner, too.'

'We'll go to work on him this evening.'

'Really? . . . And who else did you dance with?'

'Well I think it's disgusting!'

Still, it'll probably be all right in the end!

'Gretna Green? . . . don't tell me that old place is still going!'

PEOPLE AT HOME

A POOL IN THE GARDEN

'Gibson—my children
  met yours at a
  party.'

'She did a length—
  butterfly!'

'Exactly where is this beetle?'

'I never knew they had so many friends.'

NEWLY ON THE MARKET

'... *and this is the spare bedroom.*'

'*I almost forgot to show you the patio.*'

'Just wait till you see this rockery.'

'Now you could comfortably get a single bed in there.'

'So much for the kitchen.'

'A pony for the kids—is that what you're thinking?'

*'You'll have to decide quickly—I've a bank manager and
his wife absolutely crazy about it.'*

A CLEAR OUT IN THE GARAGE

'Good heavens! There's a window here!'

'I always wondered where this hat got to!'

'Anything around the place we could paint birch grey?'

'The old Talbot!'

*'Of **course** I remember, Mummy.'*

'There's some stuff for softening old paint-brushes, isn't there?'

'Yes, that's it—the Suez Crisis! We put a little by.'

'I say, doesn't it make the car look tiny!'

PEOPLE NEXT DOOR

A TOUCH OF WINTER

'You can put that one on for a start!'

*'You're never going to walk up
Cannon Street like that!'*

'That draught excluder hasn't been much of a success.'

STATION

THE
RINGING TONE

*'Penny Fulbright wants to know if you got 23 gallons
as the answer to problem number seven.'*

'Do hurry dear! . . . I want to ring Granny.'

'Barchester 7529.'

'Speaking!'

'Good heavens no! . . . of course
I'll keep it to myself old man!'

'It's for you!'

'D'you fancy a mustard-coloured
fisherman's-knit turtle-necked
sweater?'

57

'Miss Benson's out . . . this is her sitter speaking.'

'Can you call back? . . . He's lying down for an hour.'

'What sort of funny wheezing noise . . . ?'

'Clive send his love, too.'

FATHER'S DAY

'Father's Day starts at nine-fifteen!'

'It seemed an appropriate day to bring him along to meet them.'

'By God, this is one Father's Day I'll **never** forget!'

'No Charlie —not today!'

'Good heavens . . . is it really?'

'I don't remember us opening a bottle of champagne on Mothering Sunday!'

'Seeing it's Father's Day you're taking us all out to dinner.'

A WEEK WITH THE PAINTERS

'All right . . . I'll manage . . .'

'Honestly, the time it takes some
people to have a bath.'

'They've been looking everywhere for that!'

'Mrs. Taylor always gave us chocolate-covered digestives.'